Painted Ladies

butterflies of north america

by

millie miller
and
cyndi nelson

Johnson Books

Boulder

©19

an

GW00459327

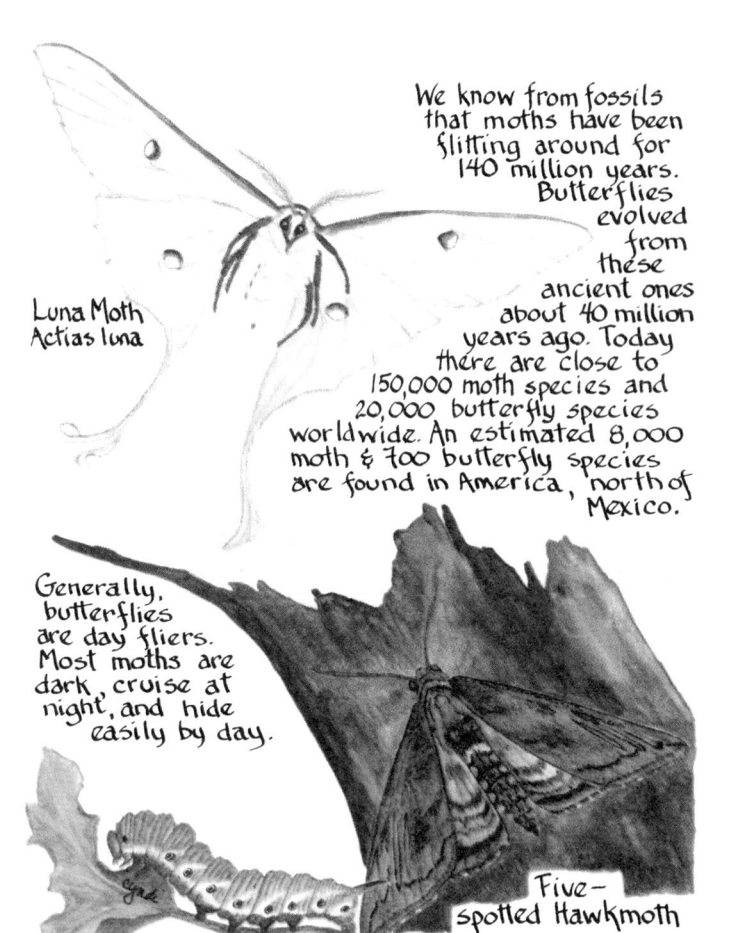

We know from fossils that moths have been flitting around for 140 million years. Butterflies evolved from these ancient ones about 40 million years ago. Today there are close to 150,000 moth species and 20,000 butterfly species worldwide. An estimated 8,000 moth & 700 butterfly species are found in America, north of Mexico.

Luna Moth
Actias luna

Generally, butterflies are day fliers. Most moths are dark, cruise at night, and hide easily by day.

Five-spotted Hawkmoth
Manduca quinquemaculata

Tomato Hornworm

Butterflies are apt to perch with wings proudly clapped over their back, whereas moths tend to rest with their wings outstretched. Generally, butterflies have knobs at the end of their antennae while moths usually have feathery or threadlike hooked antennae.

Isabella Moth

Pyrrharctia isabella

Wooly Bear Caterpillar

Spicebush Butterfly caterpillar & chrysalis.

Hemileuca maia

Often moth caterpillars are furry, while several butterfly caterpillars are smooth & green. Both may be armed with stinging spines, smelly horns, or huge "false eyes" for protection.

Some adult moths actually have no mouths & live their entire (but short) lives off their plump bodies.

Usually butterflies have naked chrysalises while many moths have the extra protection of silk cocoons.

Buck Moth

Luna Moth Cocoon

Flutterbys

Males often go "puddling"... a gathering at wet muddy places to get necessary salt for mating, a "salty butter" passed on to females. Dung heaps, carrion, or salty people may also be visited by "the fellas" for the same reason. Moths haunt these places by night.

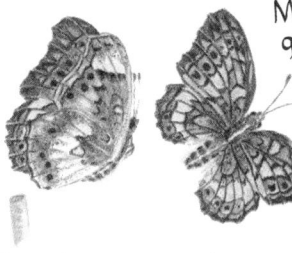

Though compound eyes cannot make out detail, they can see "hidden" ultraviolet colors in other b'flies (to distinguish sex &/or species) & in special UV flowers (for favorite nectar).

On mornings, cloudy days, or when temp is below 80° F., "basking" is essential

... to warm up flight muscles. Wings are spread open or folded toward the sun to absorb heat.

Long double-tubed tongue (proboscis) uncoils to drink the depths of flower nectar, rotten fruit, dung, or other x-rated fluids.

A male's search for females (from a perch or active patrol) is lifelong. Some court with touching or unique flutterings. Mating happens often, (and it's a short life!) can last from 10 minutes to hours, & may even occur in tandem flight. Mated females then reject other suitors.

Butterflies & moths belong to the order Lepidoptera which means "scaly wings" & are the only insects covered with scales (flattened hairs). These are arranged like overlapping shingles on a roof & have many uses.

Pigmented scales show solid colors (males tend to be more colorful) whereas prismlike scales reflect light, making iridescent hues.

Black scales help absorb heat. Some male butterflies even have sex scales that produce hormones (pheromones) which function like "perfume" during courtship. Some scale patterns camouflage or warn of distastefulness. Brushaway scales come off easily aiding escape & dusting predators.

Antennae are for smelling.

WS ½"

SMALL BLUE

FOREWING

HINDWING

ABDOMEN

THORAX

WS 11"
QUEEN
ALEXANDRA

Egg-laying females usually fly low, first looking, then smelling, & finally tasting with their feet for the right plant... their life's goal. A few even sprinkle the grass with their eggs.

"...such stuff as dreams are made of..."

Butterflies etc. in this book are not necessarily drawn to scale.

The average lifespan of an adult is around 2 weeks although some cold-climate species take up to 2 years to go from egg to adult.

Butterflies & moths change from eggs to caterpillars (larvae) to chrysalises (pupae) to adults... magic known as metamorphosis. Broods of hundreds of eggs may be laid singly or in rows, strands, or clusters, usually on or near the host plant. Generally, more broods are laid in the South ... some even year round. Eggs vary in size, shape, & color, sometimes darkening with time depending on the species.

The first thing a caterpillar does after hatching is to eat its nourishing egg shell with its large mouth. Then these "eating machines" can go on to devour mass quantities of vegetation.

Caterpillars have 5 stages called INSTARS, in between which they shed their skins to grow bigger (molt). For the final molt, they pick a good base to rest on & eat no more (or pupate).

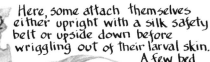

Here, some attach themselves either upright with a silk safety belt or upside down before wriggling out of their larval skin. A few bed down in silken leaf rolls. A new skin quickly hardens over the caterpillar, encasing the miraculous changes inside as the body is broken down into a thick yellowish liquid.

These pupae or chrysalises, formed in different shapes & colors, are often brownish green.

Finally it crawls out, takes in air and hangs upside down, allowing fluid to fill the wing veins quickly so the wings will expand fully before they dry & harden.

(Moths usually add the protection of a silken cocoon.)

Eventually the chrysalis hints at the forming of wings, body & head of the surfacing adult inside. When the butterfly is fully formed, it pumps fluids from its abdomen into its thorax and head, splitting open the chrysalis.

These most brilliant births are often early in the day, using the help of the morning sun. It takes an hour or more for the wings to fully dry.. skykissers at last!

milkweed

cindy

Metamorphosis...

rights of passage.

Butterflies are cold blooded & need the SUN'S WARMTH to fly. Heat also enables eggs & caterpillars to grow faster.

B'flies will linger longer in a QUIET SPOT buffered from kids & pets.

For a close-up view, entice them with a brew of stale beer, overripe fruit mash, molasses, sugar, fruit juice, & water. Spread generously on tree trunks & rocks or serve on a soaked rag or sponge. Simple rotten bananas work well if you're not into brewing.

Butterfly gardens can be anything from a window box to a meadow.

lantana

Miata

They need SHELTER from the storm...trees & hedges create calm nooks. As clouds hide the sun, in anticipation of battering rain-drops, they swiftly take refuge under leaves, blossoms, grass blades, woody surfaces, & rocks.

Create a nice MUD PUDDLE... butterflies need wetness rather than water.

Wet Sands
PUDDLING BAR

Happy Day !!!

My lilac bush was in full bloom, my daisies were in bud, & I had just finished planting my marigolds.

I stood up to view my garden with a discriminating eye & decided the milkweed near the fence had to go. As I dug in my shovel, a huge orange butterfly lighted on the topmost blossom. With bated breath, I watched my guest...enchanted. I gently leaned my shovel against the fence & surveyed my garden with new interest.

For the next few days, I scouted out the flowers & visiting butterflies not only in my garden but also in parks, roadways, & vacant lots of the neighborhood. Moving in SLOW MOTION, I could come close enough to sketch a likeness of the butterflies & their FAVORITE PLANTS. Time well spent!

Treat yourself to unhurried time with the butterflies you have invited to your garden. Discover eggs, observe the growth of caterpillars, & marvel at these bright-winged gypsies.

Contact the
LEPIDOPTERISTS' SOCIETY or the
XERCES SOCIETY

to share the excitement of a rekindled youth.

Check with your library or bookstore for more information on how to study b'flies.

Collect on film, not on pins.

Bloomin' Butterflies

Rainforest & native habitats are dwindling so even the tiniest butterfly garden helps.

Your concern makes the biggest difference of all.

Garden Varieties

Caterpillars gorge on **HOST PLANTS** while butterflies dine on **NECTAR PLANTS**. In creating a butterfly garden be sure to know your butterflies' menu.   Here are a few general butterfly favorites:

Trees & shrubs... aspen/poplar, cottonwood, plum, hackberry, willow, butterfly bush, lilac, honeysuckle, privet, and spice bush.

Flowers... alfalfa, yarrow, milkweed, aster, black-sunflower, purple coneflower, daisy, lantana, bee balm, borage, mint, Joe-Pye-weed, red valerian, lavender, blazing star, daylily, rosemary, flowering tobacco, petunia, zinnia, marigold, stonecrop, goldenrod, pincushion, coreopsis, and verbena.

eyed Susan,

Cabbage, broccoli, Japanese honeysuckle vine, & many grasses.

In planning your garden, no matter what your style, consider that often some part of a butterfly's life cycle might need to overwinter undisturbed in last year's plant growth. A more natural setting is less work for you & preferred by many butterflies (who also request **NO CHEMICALS**, PLEASE).

Caretake by pinching back & deadheading faded flowers as this usually encourages more blossoms.

Obtain from nurseries or friends **NATIVE PLANTS** that overlap blooming seasons.

You might offer a hibernation box for wintering adults.

Mimicry

Whether you make one or buy it, line it with slabs of bark & mount in a shady spot.

Caterpillars & butterflies are masters of mime... their survival depends on it. Caterpillars mimic bird droppings, fierce snakes, or project evil-looking "tongues" that emit noxious odors to frighten away predators.

Some yummy-tasting butterflies copy the colors & patterns of yukky ones to escape being someone's next meal.

Butterflies also camouflage as leaves or bark. Others have fake antennae or eyespots on their tails to fool birds into biting the "wrong end."

purple coneflower

LIFESTYLE... 2 or more broods. Up to 500 eggs laid one at a time... poor thing!

Caterpillar resembles bird droppings, has red scent "horns" & provokes citrus farmers.

Largest North American butterfly.

HOST... citrus & related prickly-ash & hoptree.

Heraclides cresphontes

Giant

WS 3½– 5½"

NECTAR... citrus flowers, lantana, lilac, honeysuckle, azalea, bougainvillea, & goldenrod.

FAVORS... open streamsides & glades.

A "high flier."

Mimics pipevine

WS 3½– 4½"

Spicebush

Pterourus troilus

LIFESTYLE... 2-4 broods. Winters as chrysalis. Female bluer than male.

NECTAR... honeysuckle, clover, azalea, jewelweed, milkweed, Joe-Pye, & thistle.

HOST... bays, spice-bush, & sassafras.

FAVORS... woodlands.

LIFESTYLE... 1-3 broods. Young brown caterpillar matures to big-eye green "snake." Winters as sticklike chrysalis. Males gather at mud puddles.

Tiger

FAVORS... at home most everywhere.

HOST... broadleaf trees/shrubs, cherries, poplars, birches, & willows.

Pterourus glaucus
WS 3-5½"

Dark female mimics pipevine in the South.

NECTAR... B'fly bush, thistle, clover, honeysuckle, bee-balm, milkweed, sunflower, dandelion, etc.

Battus philenor

Pipevine
WS 2¾-3½"

LIFESTYLE... 2-3 broods. Orange eggs in clusters. Caterpillar has scent "horns." Winters as chrysalis. Model for several mimics.

HOST... noxious tasting pipevines, Dutchmans pipe, & Virginia snakeroot, making adults bad tasting to predators.

Spread of pipevine has expanded its range.

NECTAR... azalea, thistle, lilac, milkweed, b'fly bush, phlox, orchid, honeysuckle, clover, petunia, & fruit tree blossoms.

FAVORS... open areas.

Largest & best known. Most have characteristic tails. Many caterpillars can protrude hidden orange, fleshy scent "horns" to emit noxious odor when threatened.

Swallowtails...

Parnassius phoebus
Phoebus' Parnassian

LIFESTYLE...
One brood of button-shaped white eggs. Winters as smooth tan chrysalis, protected by loose cocoon in grass or debris. Possibly takes 2 years to butterfly. Parnassian more primitive than true swallowtails, lacking tails & scent "horns." Diverse markings. Darker coloration in colder climes to absorb more heat. After mating, male seals female with a gray, waxy, pouchlike chastity belt (sphragis).

FAVORS... Montane to Alpine meadows. May fly in snowstorms.

HOST... stonecrops.
NECTAR... stonecrop & butterweeds.

♂

♀

WS
2⅛ - 3½"

Stonecrop

Millie

...especially for B.D.

Anise   Papilio zelicaon

WS 2½-3½"
Males gather
on hilltops &
at mud puddles to
girl watch.

FAVORS...
Adaptable.
At home in all
open spaces, even
vacant city lots.
Avoids heavy woods.

NECTAR...zinnias,
penstemon, mint, &
butterfly bush.

Protective eyespot.

Winters
as chrysalis.
LIFESTYLE... 1 or
more broods.
Yellow eggs.
Most common
swallowtail
west of Rockies.

HOST... leaves
& flowers of
fennel, parsley,
cow parsnips,
carrot & citrus.

LIFESTYLE... 2-4 broods.
Green eggs.
FAVORS... Wet areas &
waterside walks.
Common along
Potomic River.
Avoids suburbs.
Roosts in
groups.
Late
broods
larger & darker.

HOST...pawpaw plant.
NECTAR...variable.
Likes composites.

Eurytides
marcellus
Zebra

Winters as
chrysalis.

Longest-tailed
N.A.
swallow-
tail is
variable
in size,
stripe
width,
& tail
length.

WS 2¼-4"

Zinnia

Millie

...more swallowtails

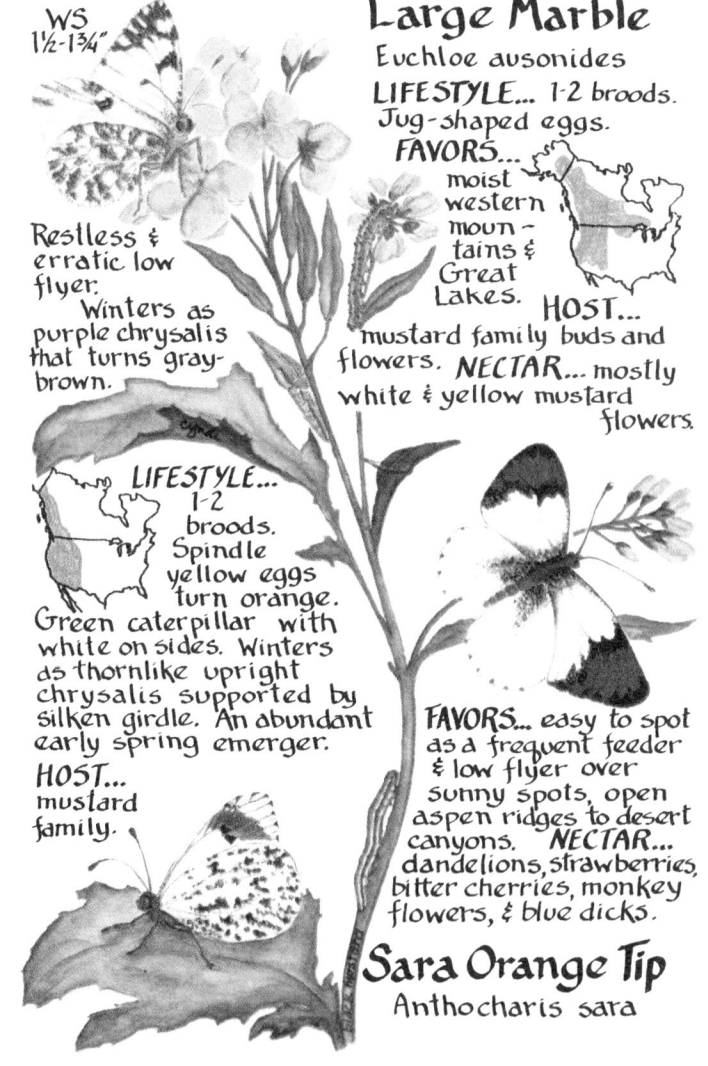

WS
1½-1¾"

Large Marble
Euchloe ausonides
LIFESTYLE... 1-2 broods.
Jug-shaped eggs.
FAVORS... moist western mountains & Great Lakes.
HOST... mustard family buds and flowers. **NECTAR...** mostly white & yellow mustard flowers.

Restless & erratic low flyer.
Winters as purple chrysalis that turns gray-brown.

LIFESTYLE... 1-2 broods. Spindle yellow eggs turn orange. Green caterpillar with white on sides. Winters as thornlike upright chrysalis supported by silken girdle. An abundant early spring emerger.

HOST... mustard family.

FAVORS... easy to spot as a frequent feeder & low flyer over sunny spots, open aspen ridges to desert canyons. **NECTAR...** dandelions, strawberries, bitter cherries, monkey flowers, & blue dicks.

Sara Orange Tip
Anthocharis sara

Checkered
Pontia protodice

LIFESTYLE... several broods. Yellow spindle-shaped eggs. Caterpillars and chrysalises have black speckles on blue-green.

Winters as chrysalis.

♂ Summer male whitest.

WS 1¼-2"
♀

FAVORS... can be abundant in scraggly open spaces.

HOST... mustards and bee plants.

NECTAR... mustard, milkweed, & aster.

Cabbage
Pieris rapae   WS 1¼-2"

LIFESTYLE... one of earliest spring emergers. Male has 1 spot on FW, female has 2.

FAVORS... introduced to Quebec from Europe in 1860. Soon everywhere except very cold climes. Now some gardeners consider a pest.

HOST... mustards including cabbage & nasturtiums.

NECTAR... host plants plus dandelion, red clover, & many others.

Several broods, darkening through summer.

Yellow vase-shaped eggs.

Winters as thorny, green chrysalis.

Caterpillar can change hues to hide.

Whites & sulphers both have seasonal & sexual differences in coloration. Fond of puddling.

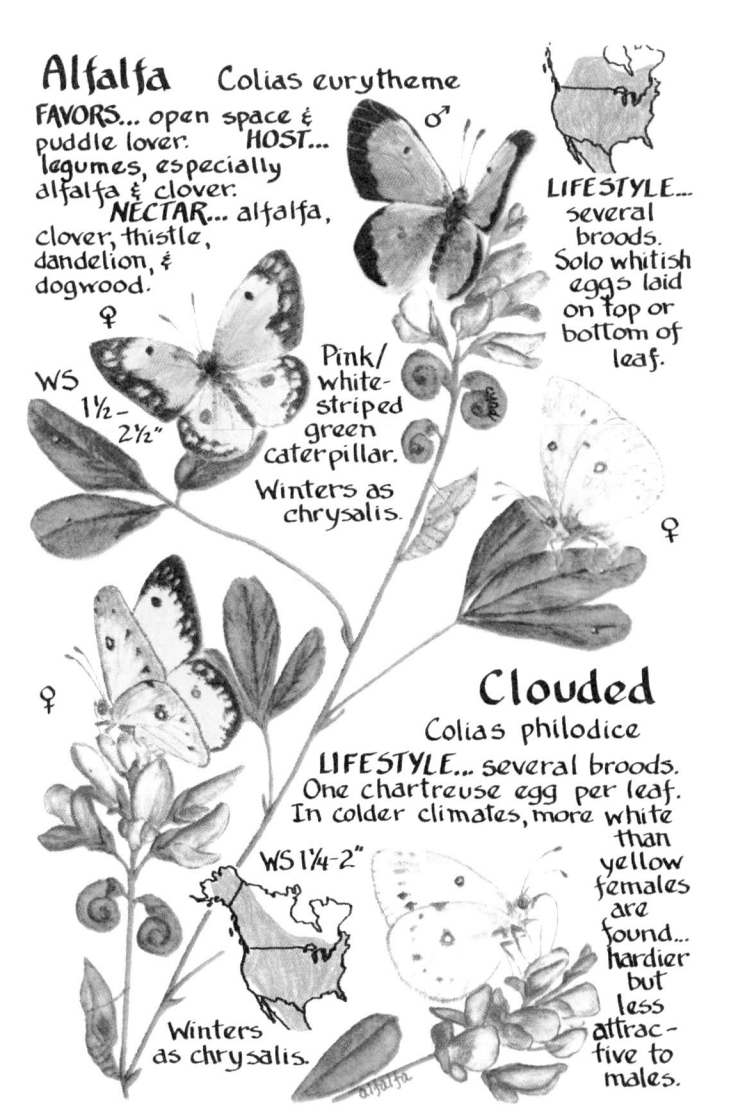

Alfalfa
Colias eurytheme

FAVORS... open space & puddle lover. **HOST...** legumes, especially alfalfa & clover.
   NECTAR... alfalfa, clover, thistle, dandelion, & dogwood.

♂

LIFESTYLE... several broods. Solo whitish eggs laid on top or bottom of leaf.

♀

WS 1½ – 2½"

Pink/white-striped green caterpillar.

Winters as chrysalis.

♀

Clouded
Colias philodice

LIFESTYLE... several broods. One chartreuse egg per leaf. In colder climates, more white than yellow females are found... hardier but less attractive to males.

WS 1¼-2"

Winters as chrysalis.

alfalfa

FAVORS... open spaces.

"Mud puddle" males congregate at local wet spots.

The higher the elevation or the earlier the brood, the darker the underwing for better heat absorption. **HOST...** legumes, especially clovers & alfalfa. **NECTAR...** goldenrod, clover, phlox, & milkweed.

Dogface
Zerene cesonia

LIFESTYLE... 3 or more broods. Yellow-green eggs (turning crimson) laid singly on underside of host leaf.

California Dogface cousin known as "Flying Pansy." These "poodle-heads" have "rosa" flush in winter. **FAVORS...** lives in open woodlands, arid areas, or most anywhere. Young bucks at puddles watch all the girls go by. **HOST...** false indigo & clover.

NECTAR... clovers, thistles, verbena, & blue dicks.

Black/yellow stripes vary on caterpillar.

Female sometimes white.

WS 1¾-2½"

Winters as chrysalis or adult.

Sulphurs...

Dainty
Nathalis iole

"Lemon drop" eggs laid singly on seedling leaves.

Emerald caterpillar has purple, black, & yellow stripes.

WS ½-1¼"

♀

Smooth, green chrysalis lacks "head horn".

Females wear more black.

NECTAR... marigolds, weedy composites, & pinks. Many fly north from Mexico to Canada, only to die in the cold.

LIFESTYLE... many broods in South all year.

FAVORS... often seen traveling up river, along roadsides, or riding the rails.

HOST... marigolds, chickweed, & sneezeweed.

Smallest sulphur in North America.

Cloudless Sulphur
Phoebis sennae

LIFESTYLE... many broods in South. White pitcher-shaped eggs turn pale orange.

Caterpillar hides out by day in silk and leaf tent. Males clear yellow & may be mottled below.

♂

WS 2-2¾"

FAVORS... open, sunny areas and shores. Named for **HOST...** sennas, also wild pea

candi

senna

and clovers.

NECTAR... lantana, hibiscus, bougainvillea, & morning glory. The mystery of these giants is their mass, fatal emigration northward every fall.

Adults overwinter in South.

more Sulphurs...

Not a true
copper
but
related.

Harvester
Feniseca tarquinius
LIFESTYLE...several broods.
Have short 3-week lifespan.

Mint-colored eggs
laid singly among aphids.

HOST...
wooly
aphids.

Winters
as green-brown caterpillar buried
in blanket of dead aphids. Monkey-
face on back of chrysalis.

One of a kind in North
America, having
tropical cousins.

FAVORS...prefers
moist places
with alder, beech,
& witch hazel.

NECTAR..."honey dew,"
a polite name for
aphid
secretions.

WS
1-1¼"

beech

Only North
American carnivore.

Purplish Copper

Epidemia helloides

LIFESTYLE... many broods. Whitish eggs. Caterpillar green with yellow stripes. Winters as greenish chrysalis.

Hardy...seen in late fall.

WS 1-1¼"

FAVORS... wet areas, sea level to 10,000'.

HOST... buckwheats such as docks, sorrels, & knotweeds. Sometimes cinquefoil.

NECTAR... dock & baby's breath.

curly dock

Little Copper

Lycaena phlaeas

LIFESTYLE... 2+ broods. Ribbed pale green eggs. Furry little green or rosy caterpillar. Winters as chrysalis. Summer adults emerge darker than spring forms.

FAVORS... brightens disturbed areas.
HOST... sorrel & dock.
NECTAR... daisies, butterfly weed, goldenrod, & yarrow.

WS ¾-1½"

Gossamer Wings... include coppers, blues, hairstreaks, elfins, & the harvester. All bask with wings folded toward sun. Metalmark cousins bask with flat wings.

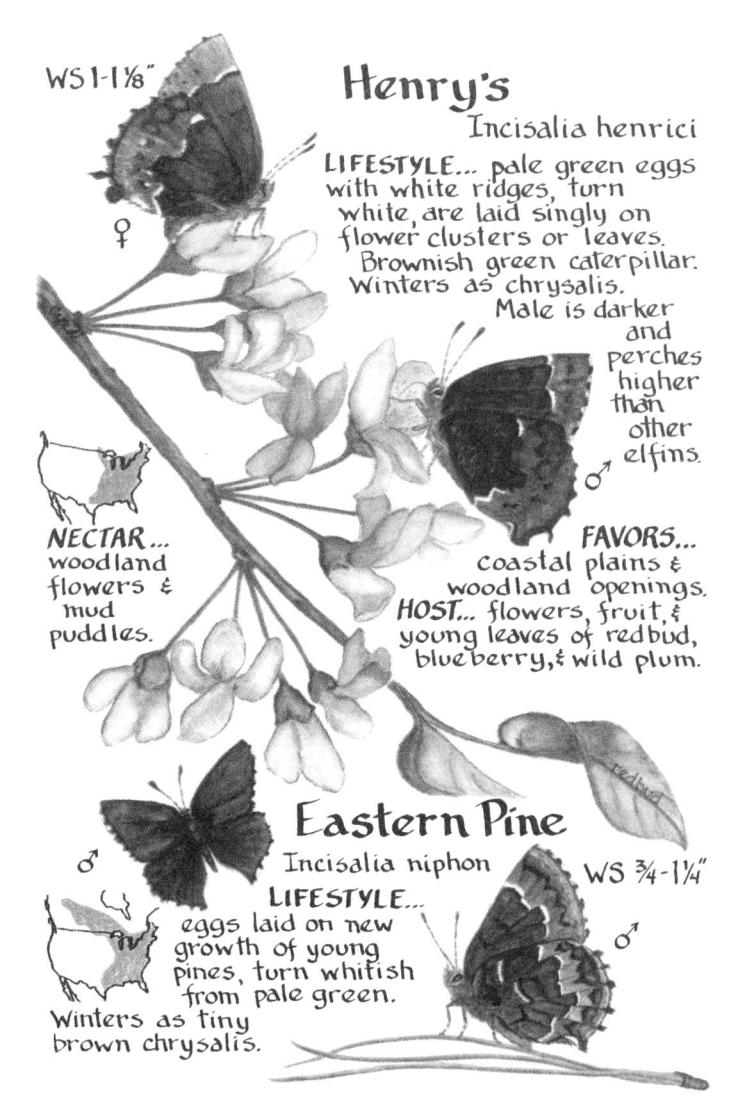

WS 1-1⅛"

♀

Henry's
Incisalia henrici

LIFESTYLE... pale green eggs with white ridges, turn white, are laid singly on flower clusters or leaves. Brownish green caterpillar. Winters as chrysalis. Male is darker and perches higher than other elfins.

♂

NECTAR... woodland flowers & mud puddles.

FAVORS... coastal plains & woodland openings. **HOST...** flowers, fruit, & young leaves of redbud, blueberry, & wild plum.

redbud

♂

Eastern Pine
Incisalia niphon

WS ¾-1¼"

♂

LIFESTYLE... eggs laid on new growth of young pines, turn whitish from pale green. Winters as tiny brown chrysalis.

FAVORS... both native & ornamental pines.
HOST... young pine needles. NECTAR... late
emerging adults feed on wild plum,
dogbane, lupine, everlasting,
& other
wildflowers.

♀

Western Pine
Incisalia eryphon

♂

WS ¾ - 1¼"
Male
chocolate
above.

♀

HOST...
young
pine
needles.

NECTAR.
pussy
willows,
lupines,
and
many
wild
flowers.

LIFESTYLE... single
white eggs. Rich-green
caterpillar with creamy
stripes. Winters as brown
chrysalis. FAVORS... prefers
bogs & meadows of native pine
forests up to 10,000'. Hitchhikes
on Christmas trees to expand
territory east.

Elfins have 1 brood. Females are larger and
brighter. All males except Henry's have sex
spot on forewings.

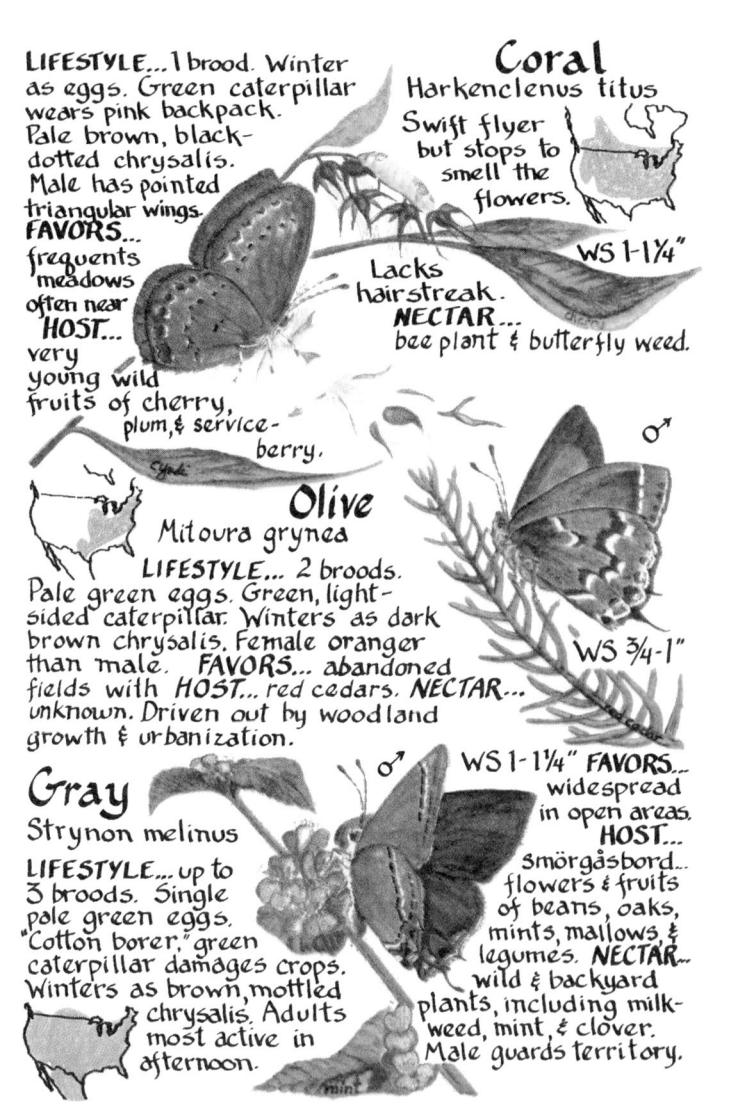

Coral

Harkenclenus titus

Swift flyer but stops to smell the flowers.

WS 1-1¼"

LIFESTYLE... 1 brood. Winter as eggs. Green caterpillar wears pink backpack. Pale brown, black-dotted chrysalis. Male has pointed triangular wings. **FAVORS...** frequents meadows often near **HOST...** very young wild fruits of cherry, plum, & service-berry.

Lacks hairstreak.

NECTAR... bee plant & butterfly weed.

Olive

Mitoura grynea

LIFESTYLE... 2 broods. Pale green eggs. Green, light-sided caterpillar. Winters as dark brown chrysalis. Female oranger than male. **FAVORS...** abandoned fields with **HOST...** red cedars, **NECTAR...** unknown. Driven out by woodland growth & urbanization.

♂

WS ¾-1"

Gray

Strynon melinus

LIFESTYLE... up to 3 broods. Single pale green eggs. "Cotton borer," green caterpillar damages crops. Winters as brown, mottled chrysalis. Adults most active in afternoon.

♂

WS 1-1¼" **FAVORS...** widespread in open areas. **HOST...** smörgåsbord... flowers & fruits of beans, oaks, mints, mallows & legumes. **NECTAR...** wild & backyard plants, including milk-weed, mint, & clover. Male guards territory.

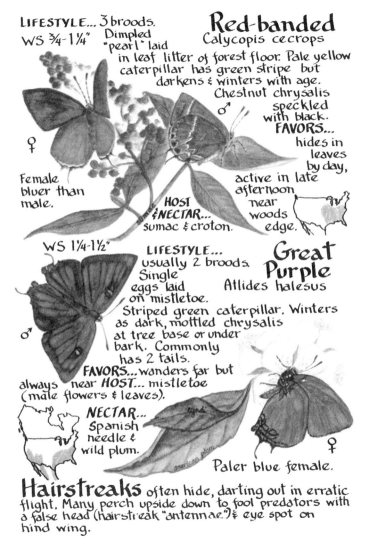

Red-banded
Calycopis cecrops

LIFESTYLE... 3 broods.
WS ¾-1¼" Dimpled "pearl" laid in leaf litter of forest floor. Pale yellow caterpillar has green stripe but darkens & winters with age. Chestnut chrysalis speckled with black.

FAVORS... hides in leaves by day, active in late afternoon near woods edge.

♀

Female bluer than male.

♂

HOST & NECTAR... sumac & croton.

Great Purple
Atlides halesus

WS 1¼-1½"

LIFESTYLE... usually 2 broods. Single eggs laid on mistletoe. Striped green caterpillar. Winters as dark, mottled chrysalis at tree base or under bark. Commonly has 2 tails.

♂

FAVORS... wanders far but always near **HOST...** mistletoe (male flowers & leaves).

NECTAR... Spanish needle & wild plum.

♀

Paler blue female.

Hairstreaks
often hide, darting out in erratic flight. Many perch upside down to fool predators with a false head (hairstreak "antennae") & eye spot on hind wing.

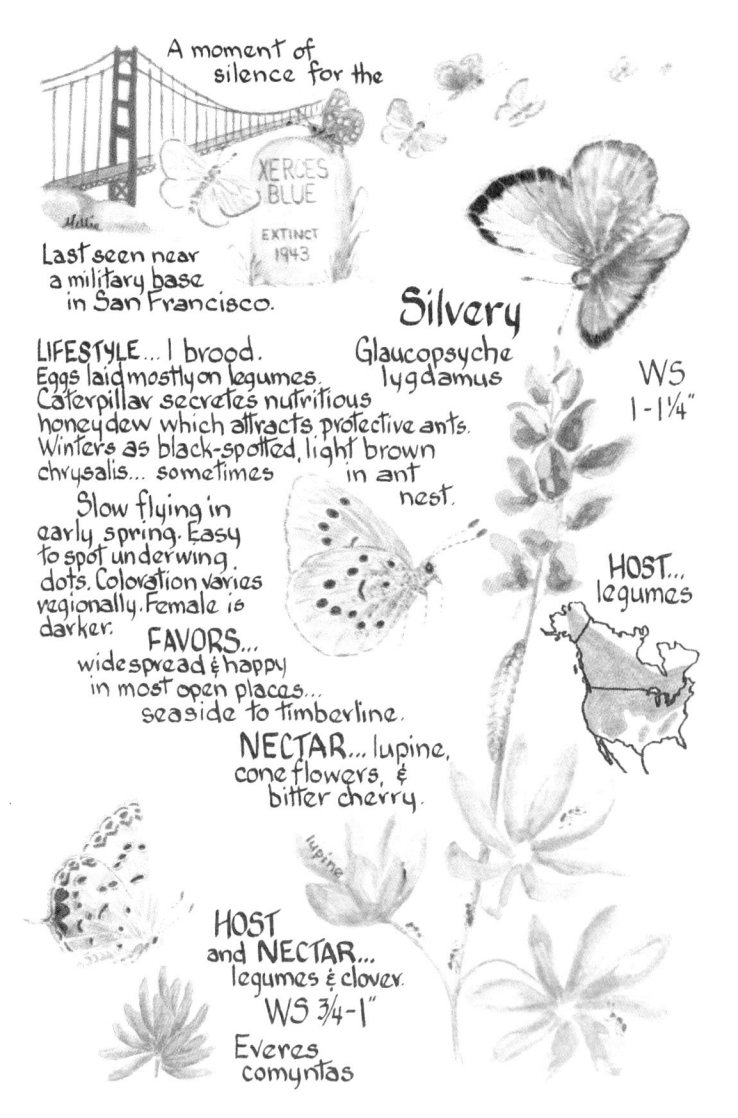

A moment of silence for the

XERCES BLUE
EXTINCT 1943

Last seen near a military base in San Francisco.

Silvery
Glaucopsyche lygdamus

WS 1 - 1¼"

LIFESTYLE... 1 brood. Eggs laid mostly on legumes. Caterpillar secretes nutritious honeydew which attracts protective ants. Winters as black-spotted, light brown chrysalis... sometimes in ant nest.

Slow flying in early spring. Easy to spot underwing dots. Coloration varies regionally. Female is darker.

FAVORS... widespread & happy in most open places... seaside to timberline.

NECTAR... lupine, cone flowers, & bitter cherry.

HOST... legumes

lupine

HOST and NECTAR... legumes & clover.
WS ¾-1"

Everes comyntas

Eastern Tailed

LIFESTYLE... 3 broods. Pale green eggs laid singly. Over-winters in legume pods as green caterpillar. Creamy chrysalis. Has larger western cousin. Females bluer in spring.

FAVORS... Abundant & low-flying. Thrives in disturbed areas.

red clover

Millie

LIFESTYLE... 1-3 broods. Pea-green eggs deposited on flower buds in dogwood & other trees. Caterpillar usually creamy with green stripes, sometimes mottled pink.

Winters as yellow-brown chrysalis. Heralds spring. Early broods darker blue. May only live 4 days. Males actively patrol for females. **FAVORS...** Woodlands from sea level to mountains.

♂

♂

dogwood

HOST... varies with season from dogwood, viburnum, to blueberry.

Spring Azure
Celastrina argiolus
WS ¾-1¼"

NECTAR... early spring flowers like rockcress, dandelion, & cherry.

Males puddle.

♀

Ants milk a rich sugar & protein honeydew secretion from caterpillars of some blues & hairstreaks. In exchange for this treat, ants help fend off predators...

Singin' the **Blues**

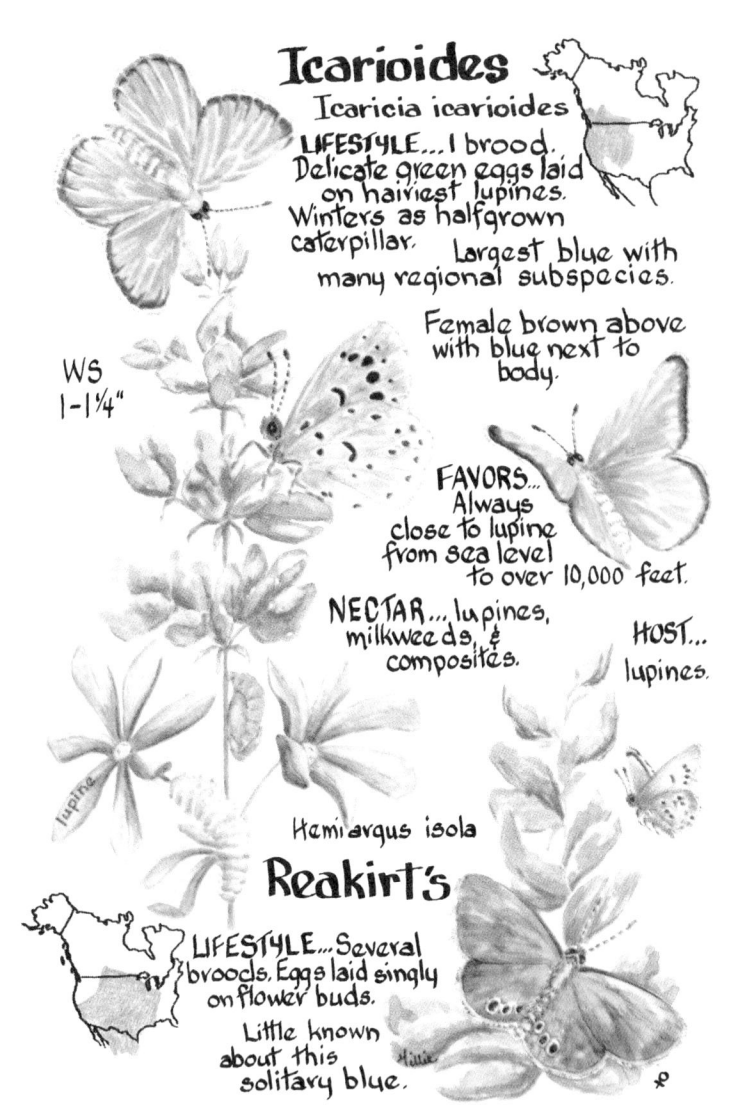

Icarioides

Icaricia icarioides

LIFESTYLE... 1 brood. Delicate green eggs laid on hairiest lupines. Winters as halfgrown caterpillar. Largest blue with many regional subspecies.

Female brown above with blue next to body.

WS
1-1¼"

FAVORS...
Always close to lupine from sea level to over 10,000 feet.

NECTAR... lupines, milkweeds, & composites.

HOST... lupines.

lupine

Hemiargus isola

Reakirt's

LIFESTYLE... Several broods. Eggs laid singly on flower buds.

Little known about this solitary blue.

Migrates north to Canada.
Males patrol host plants
for females.

FAVORS... weedy fields & open
disturbed areas.

HOST... flowers & fruits of legumes,
mesquites, & ornamental
acacias.

NECTAR... legumes
& wildflowers.

WS
¾ - 1¼"

Puddles.

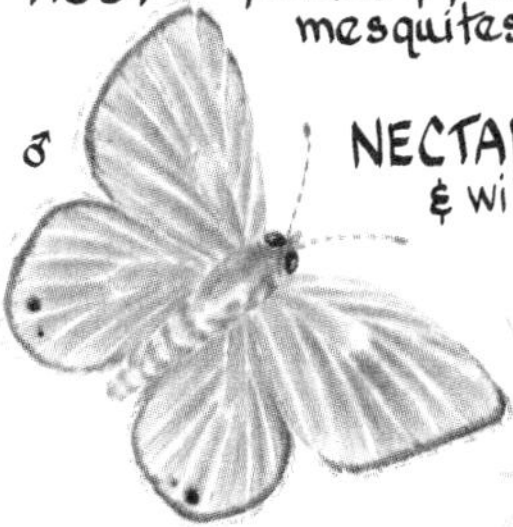

♂

Melissa

Lycaeides
melissa

WS
¾ - 1¼"

LIFESTYLE... 2-3 broods. Winter
as icy-ridged pale green eggs. Brown-
haired green caterpillar. Green
chrysalis has yellow spots. Almost
identical to Northern Blue in
overlapping ranges. Kramer
Blue cousin is protected in NY
state. FAVORS... sunny, dry,
open areas.

HOST... lupine,
alfalfa, &
wild licorice.

NECTAR...
alfalfa.

Males
puddle.

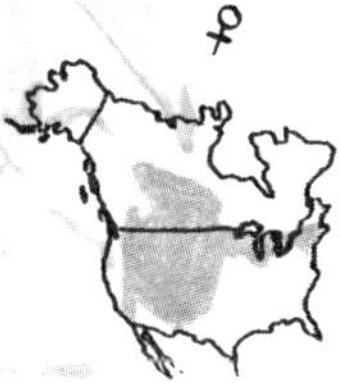

♀

♂

More of the Blues...

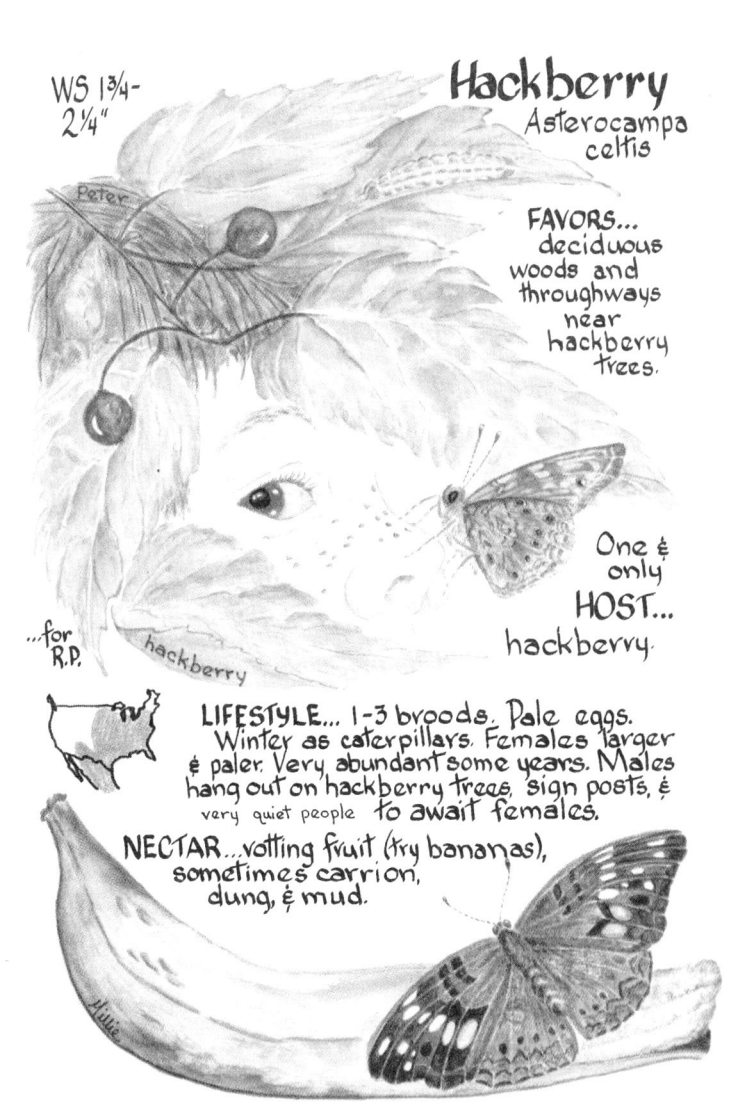

WS 1¾-2¼"

Hackberry

Asterocampa celtis

FAVORS... deciduous woods and throughways near hackberry trees.

Peter

One & only **HOST...** hackberry.

...for R.P.

hackberry

LIFESTYLE... 1-3 broods. Pale eggs. Winter as caterpillars. Females larger & paler. Very abundant some years. Males hang out on hackberry trees, sign posts, & very quiet people to await females.

NECTAR... rotting fruit (try bananas), sometimes carrion, dung, & mud.

Tropical Snout

Libytheana carinenta

NECTAR... rotting fruit, rabbit brush, peach, & dogwood. A puddler.

WS 1½-2"

LIFESTYLE... 2+ broods. Ridged, light green oval eggs. Green chrysalis. Winters as adult in South. Emigrates north en mass... a one-way trip. Snout formed by elongated mouth parts resembling leaf stem. With closed wings, camouflages self as leaf.

hackberry

HOST... fossils suggest hackberry trees for the past 30 million years.

FAVORS... canyons, draws & washes.

Mormon Metalmark

LIFESTYLE... 1 to several broods. Pale pinkish flat eggs. Winters as young caterpillar. When older, feeds by night & rests by day in a leaf nest tied with silk. Chrysalis hides in leaf litter. Swift-flying. Puffy, white spots hide metalmarks.

Often perch with open wings on underside of leaves.

Court & mate midday.

FAVORS... Camouflaged in dry rocky places.

HOST & NECTAR... buckwheats.

Little Dazzling Spots

WS ¾ - 1¼"

buckwheat

Metalmark & Snout

males walk on back four legs only.

Great Spangled

Speyeria cybele

Largest fritillary (but not related to Gulf or Atlantis).

WS 2-3"

♂

Swift fliers but take long rest stops at nectar.

Females darker above.

♀

Silver spots below.

LIFESTYLE... 1 brood. Pale yellow to brown eggs hatch in fall. Winters as unfed young caterpillar. **HOST...** spring violets. Life cycle tuned to violet bloom. **NECTAR...** thistle, milkweed, dogbane, glorisa daisy, verbena; & also dung.

Males always on the prowl for ladies. **FAVORS...** wet meadows & open woodlands.

Atlantis

Speyeria atlantis

WS 1¾-2¾" Innumerable pattern variations. Males ardently seek females (who can "smell" their own species by scent from male wings during courtship dance). **FAVORS...** moist flowery, open woodland meadows. **HOST...** violets. **NECTAR...** thistles, daisies, etc.; occasionally mud & dung.

Silver spots below.

LIFESTYLE... 1 brood. Single honey-yellow eggs. Winters as unfed, newly hatched caterpillar. Orange-spiked, purple chrysalis mottled black & brown.

A Longwing... Gulf

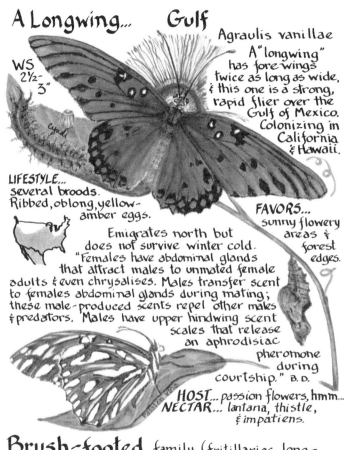

Agraulis vanillae

A "longwing" has fore wings twice as long as wide, & this one is a strong, rapid flier over the Gulf of Mexico. Colonizing in California & Hawaii.

WS 2½ - 3"

LIFESTYLE... several broods. Ribbed, oblong, yellow-amber eggs.

FAVORS... sunny flowery areas & forest edges.

Emigrates north but does not survive winter cold. "Females have abdominal glands that attract males to unmated female adults & even chrysalises. Males transfer scent to females abdominal glands during mating; these male-produced scents repel other males & predators. Males have upper hindwing scent scales that release an aphrodisiac pheromone during courtship." B.D.

HOST... passion flowers, hmm...
NECTAR... lantana, thistle, & impatiens.

Brush-footed family (fritillaries, long-wings, anglewings, tortoiseshells, thistles, admirals, sisters, satyrs, buckeye, hackberry, leafwings, crescentspots, & checkerspots) occur everywhere except the polar caps. All have short, brushy front legs & robust clubs on antennae.

Meadow
Clossiana bellona

WS 1¼-2"

LIFESTYLE... 1-3 broods.

Green-yellow eggs.

Winters as half-grown black caterpillar.

Flight is a low rapid zigzag.

Males patrol actively for females. **FAVORS...** wet meadows & pastures near woods.

Tan chrysalis.

HOST... violets.

NECTAR... Marsh flowers; also dung.

WS 1½-2"

Silver-bordered
Clossiana selene

LIFESTYLE... 1-3 broods. Creamy itsy-bitsy eggs laid near & sometimes on violets. Winters as young caterpillar.

common blue violet

enlarged eggs.

Found on all northern continents. **FAVORS...** bogs & wet meadows near woodlands. **NECTAR...** black-eyed Susans, goldenrods, & many other composites.

HOST... violets.

Variegated
Euptoieta claudia

LIFESTYLE... continuous broods, spring to fall. Ribbed creamy eggs. Winters as adult in extreme South. Low, rapid flyer.

WS 1¾-2¼"

♂

♀

FAVORS... open areas from grasslands to mountain meadows.
HOST...WIDE variety such as flax, violets, passion flower, plantain, & pansies. **NECTAR**... very broad range of flowers, including milkweed, & red clover.

Males patrol for females.

butterfly weed

Diana
Speyeria diana

♂

Species decreasing because of logging. Female mimics distasteful Pipevine. **NECTAR**... mainly milkweeds, butterfly bush, & red clover; also scat. (What's a pretty lady like you doing in a place like that?!)

WS 3-4"

LIFESTYLE... 1 brood. Eggs laid on dead leaves & twigs of forest floor. Winters as unfed black, spiny caterpillar that must find **HOST**... violets, in spring. Chrysalis red & light brown. **FAVORS**... woodlands near streams.

♀

more Fritillaries...

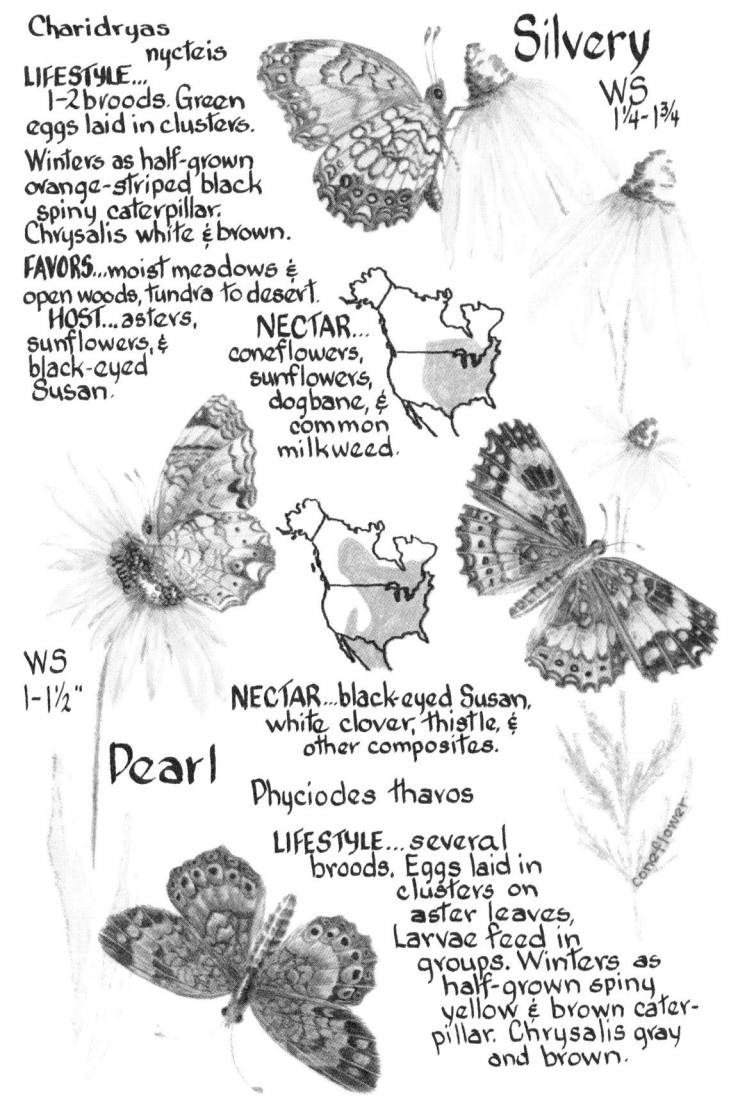

Charidryas nycteis

Silvery

WS 1¼ – 1¾

LIFESTYLE...
1-2 broods. Green eggs laid in clusters.

Winters as half-grown orange-striped black spiny caterpillar. Chrysalis white & brown.

FAVORS... moist meadows & open woods, tundra to desert.

HOST... asters, sunflowers, & black-eyed Susan.

NECTAR... coneflowers, sunflowers, dogbane, & common milkweed.

WS 1 – 1½"

NECTAR... black-eyed Susan, white clover, thistle, & other composites.

Pearl

Phyciodes thavos

LIFESTYLE... several broods. Eggs laid in clusters on aster leaves. Larvae feed in groups. Winters as half-grown spiny yellow & brown caterpillar. Chrysalis gray and brown.

coneflower

Fiesty little guys bravely check out intruders. Low-flying puddle hoppers, skimming for females.

FAVORS...open areas where asters
HOST...various are found.
smooth-leaved asters.

Very common.

LIFESTYLE... 1-3 broods.
Pale green eggs laid in clusters on asters.
Spiny cream-lined dark caterpillar feeds in groups 'til half grown, then winters alone.

Bumpy brown & cream chrysalis.

Common crescentspot in western mountains.

black-eyed Susan

Attie

Field

Phyciodes pratensis

WS 1-1½"

FAVORS...
clearings from tundra to desert.

HOST...
asters.

NECTAR...
composites.

dandelion

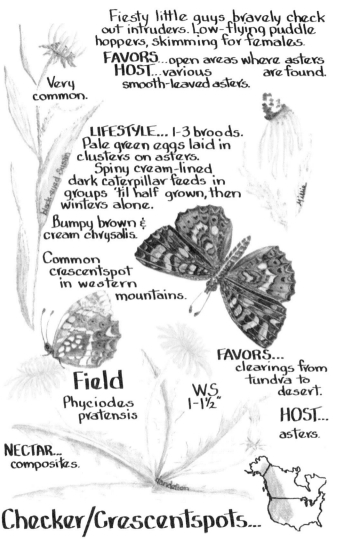

Checker/Crescentspots...

More Spots...

WS 1-1½"

LIFESTYLE...
1-3 broods. Creamy ribbed eggs laid in clusters. Feed together as young. Half-grown orange- & black- banded caterpillars winter in leaf litter. Chrysalis cream & gray. Population varies greatly year to year. Males perch on ridges & patrol hills & valleys for females.

FAVORS... grassy strips & open forests.

HOST... sunflowers, ragweed, & other weedy composites.

NECTAR...sunflowers, goldenrod, coreopsis, & white sweet clover.

Gorgone
Charidryas gorgone

Millie

sunflower

Anicia

WS 1-2"

Euphydryas anicia

FAVORS... tundra, chaparral, woodlands, & grasslands.

May defoliate **HOST...** Indian paintbrush, beardtongue, figworts, & borage, leaving silken webs.

LIFESTYLE... 1 brood. Orange eggs in clusters. Groups of spiny zebra-striped caterpillars feed together in silken nest & winter half grown. White & black chrysalis. Many variations. Also known as "Paintbrush." Pose for shutterbug.

NECTAR... bistorts & cinquefoils.

cinquefoil

LIFESTYLE... 1 brood. Winter as young caterpillars. Females twice larger than males.

FAVORS... wet woodland meadows to dry ridges near **HOST...** plantain, turtlehead, & foxglove.

NECTAR... viburnum, wild rose, & common milkweed.

WS 1½"-2½"

Named after early American Lord Baltimore whose crest was orange & black.

plantain

Euphydryas phaeton

Baltimore

Satyr

Polygonia satyrus

LIFESTYLE... 2-3 broods. Green eggs laid singly or in "short stacks" of 3 or 4. Spiny black caterpillar has green-yellow upperside. Cloaks self in leaf for shelter. Chrysalis tan & angular. Winters as adult. Basks in bright sun.

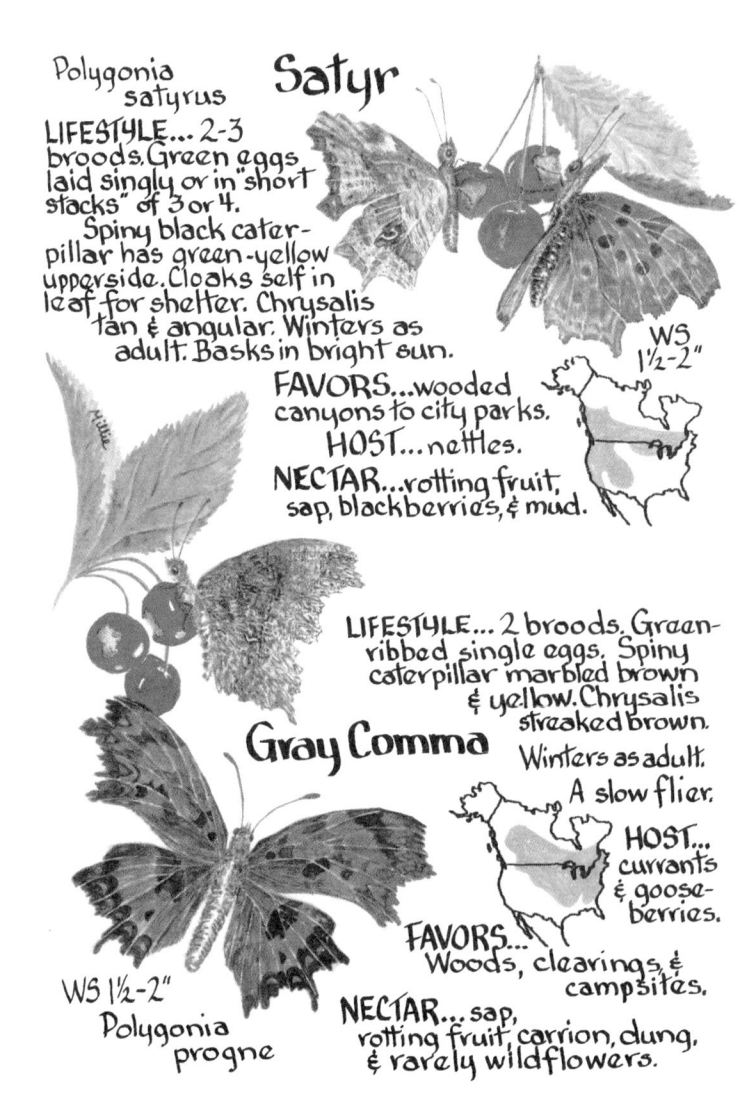

WS 1½-2"

FAVORS... wooded canyons to city parks.

HOST... nettles.

NECTAR... rotting fruit, sap, blackberries, & mud.

Gray Comma

LIFESTYLE... 2 broods. Green-ribbed single eggs. Spiny caterpillar marbled brown & yellow. Chrysalis streaked brown.

Winters as adult. A slow flier.

HOST... currants & goose-berries.

FAVORS... Woods, clearings, & campsites.

WS 1½-2"

Polygonia progne

NECTAR... sap, rotting fruit, carrion, dung, & rarely wildflowers.

Question Mark

Polygonia interrogationis

WS 2¼-2½"

LIFESTYLE... 2-4 broods. Teensy eggs. Winters as adult. Once known as "Violet Tips."

FAVORS... sunny glades & orchards. **HOST...** elm, nettle, hops & hackberries. **NECTAR...** running tree sap, carrion, dung, & rotting fruit which, if fermented, can intoxicate.

Millie

WS 1¾-2"

Hop Merchant

Polygonia comma

LIFESTYLE... 2-3 broods. Pale green "k-eggs" in columns of 2-9. Spined light green caterpillar. Chrysalis brown with speckles of gold. Winters as adult. This "Comma" lighter in fall. Pretends to attack, but say "Boo" & it will hide upside down on tree trunk.

FAVOR... Moist woodlands to suburbs. **HOST...** elms, hops, & nettles. **NECTAR...** sap, rotting fruit.

A fitting name. Hide as leaves or bark when wings closed. Winter broods darker.

Anglewings...

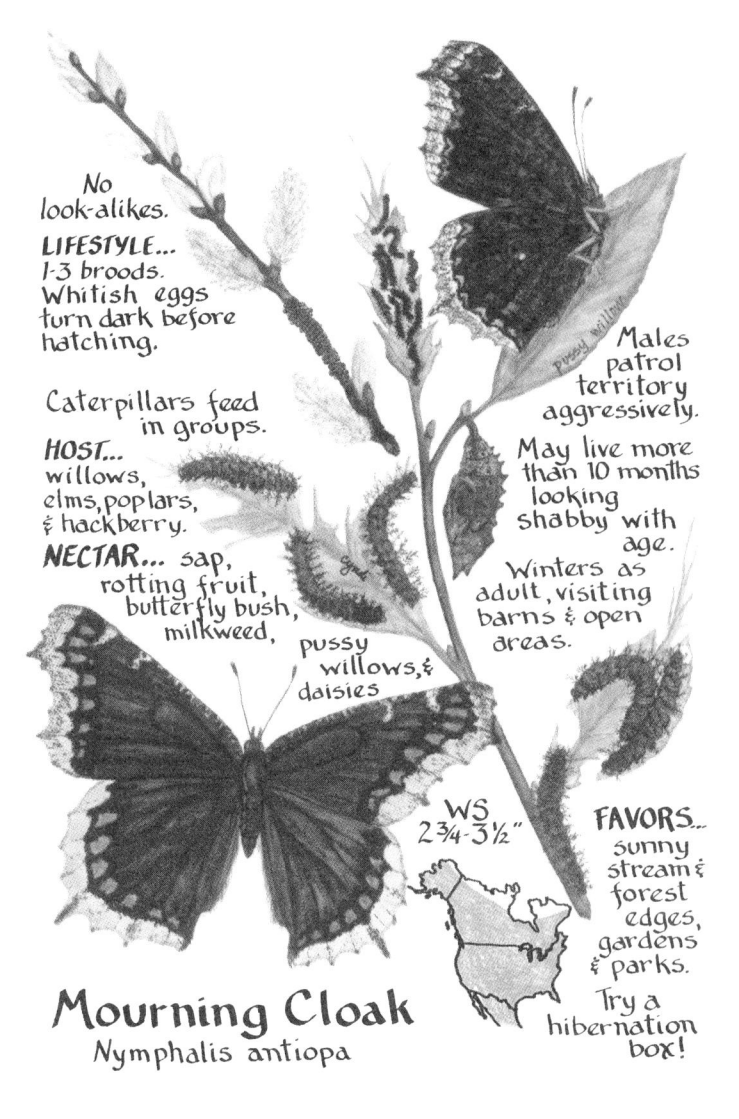

No look-alikes.

LIFESTYLE... 1-3 broods. Whitish eggs turn dark before hatching.

Caterpillars feed in groups.

HOST... willows, elms, poplars, & hackberry.

NECTAR... sap, rotting fruit, butterfly bush, milkweed, pussy willows, & daisies

pussy willow

Males patrol territory aggressively.

May live more than 10 months looking shabby with age.

Winters as adult, visiting barns & open areas.

WS 2 ¾-3 ½"

FAVORS... sunny stream & forest edges, gardens & parks.

Try a hibernation box!

Mourning Cloak
Nymphalis antiopa

FAVORS... mountains & canyons, glades & parks. Occasionally seen riding the off-season breezes.
HOST... buckhorns.
NECTAR... flowers & mud.

WS 2-2½"

butterfly bush

California

Nymphalis californica

LIFESTYLE... 1-3 broods. Eggs laid in clusters. Black velvety caterpillar. Horned gray/tan chrysalis. Winters as adult. May be rare or absent for several years & then emigrate en masse, probably because of overpopulation, food availability, & climate.

Milbert's

Aglais milberti

NECTAR... composites, butterfly bush, lilac, marigold, stonecrop, & others.

HOST... nettles & willows.
LIFESTYLE... 2-3 broods. Large masses (up to 700!) of pale green eggs. Young black & green caterpillars nest together, then solo in silken leaf roll. Winter as adult, sometimes 2 or 3 together.

WS 1¾-2"
FAVORS... at home most places.

cyndi

Tortoise Shells
resemble anglewings & are circumpolar.

Buckeye
Junonia coenia

LIFESTYLE... 2-many broods. Dark green flat-topped eggs. Snow-flecked earthy chrysalis. Flies south to winter as adult.

FAVORS... beaches & trail-like places.

NECTAR... composites & plantains. Likes to puddle or sunbathe on bare ground.

WS 2-2½"

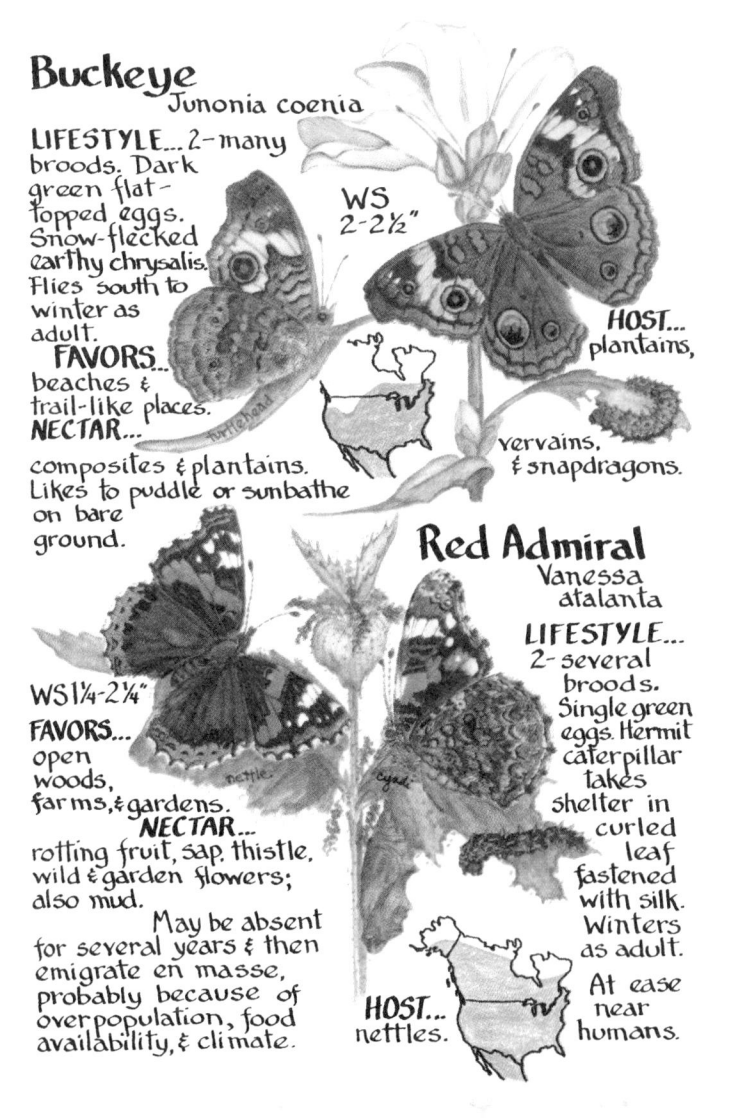

HOST... plantains, vervains, & snapdragons.

Red Admiral
Vanessa atalanta

LIFESTYLE... 2-several broods. Single green eggs. Hermit caterpillar takes shelter in curled leaf fastened with silk. Winters as adult.

WS 1¼-2¼"

FAVORS... open woods, farms, & gardens.

NECTAR... rotting fruit, sap, thistle, wild & garden flowers; also mud.

May be absent for several years & then emigrate en masse, probably because of overpopulation, food availability, & climate.

HOST... nettles.

At ease near humans.

American Painted Lady
Vanessa virginiensis

LIFESTYLE... 2-3 broods. Single pale green eggs. Winters as adult. Population varies greatly year-to-year. **FAVORS**... sunny, open, flowered fields from Alaska to Hawaii but more common in the East. Attracted by butterfly gardens & may reside in your butterfly box. **NECTAR**... composites like thistle, aster, marigold, zinnia, plus butterfly bush, vetch, & heliotrope.

WS 1¾-2¼"
The only "Lady" with 2 <u>large</u> gorgeous eye-spots on underwing.

HOST... everlastings, pussytoes, & daisy types.

ever lasting

Painted Lady
Vanessa cardui

LIFESTYLE... 2 or more broods. Single pale green "barrel" eggs. Winters as adult. This "Thistle" is a favorite in gardens worldwide because of migratory habits. Southern survivors fly north each spring to recolonize in colder climes. **FAVORS**... found everywhere. **NECTAR**... many composites, bee balm, candytuft, sweet William, & butterfly bush.

WS 2-2¼"

HOST... thistles, composites, mallow, hollyhock.

bull thistle

Thistles & Buckeye

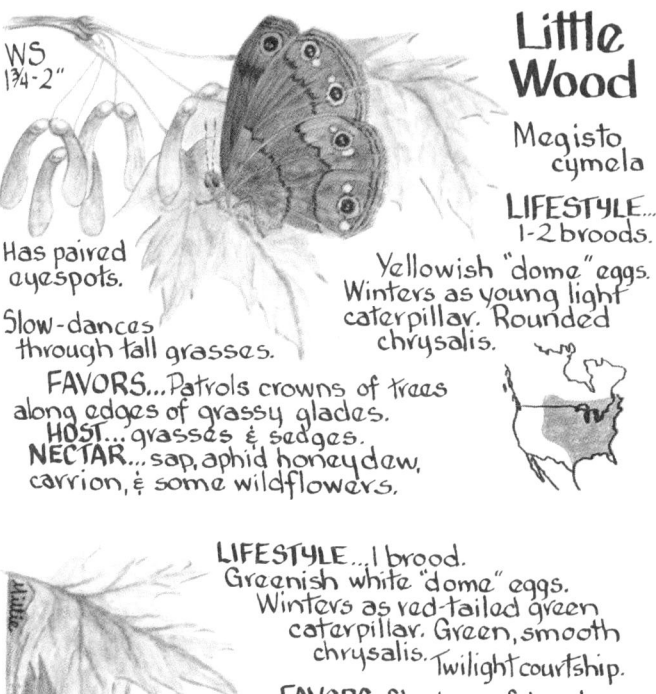

Little Wood

Megisto cymela

WS 1¾-2"

Has paired eyespots.

Slow-dances through tall grasses.

LIFESTYLE... 1-2 broods.
Yellowish "dome" eggs. Winters as young light caterpillar. Rounded chrysalis.

FAVORS... Patrols crowns of trees along edges of grassy glades.
HOST... grasses & sedges.
NECTAR... sap, aphid honeydew, carrion, & some wildflowers.

LIFESTYLE... 1 brood.
Greenish white "dome" eggs. Winters as red-tailed green caterpillar. Green, smooth chrysalis. Twilight courtship.

FAVORS... Shadows of deciduous woods, often perching upside down on tree trunks.

Northern Pearly Eye

Enodia anthedon

WS 1½-2"

HOST... grasses.
NECTAR... no flowers. Would you believe sap, mud, dung, & carrion.

Inornate Ringlet
Ceononympha tullia inornata

HOST... various grasses.

LIFESTYLE... 2 broods. Pale green barrel-shaped eggs. Winters as two-tailed green caterpillar.

On warm days, actively search for females. Play the waiting game on cooler days.

FAVORS... open prairies and meadows.

NECTAR... avid flower visitor, especially to yellow composites.

WS 1-2"

Milla   Salsify

Satyrs
characteristically adorn forest glades, meadows, & mountain tundra. Most adults stay close to home and dine lightly.

Hardiest of arctic species.

Perches on ground & leans over for thermoregulation & to camouflage itself by shadow elimination.

FAVORS... Grassy woodlands & prairies to the arctic tundra. May avoid Oregon because of 1980 Mount St. Helens eruption.

NECTAR... sip mud occasionally... rarely visit flowers.

HOST... sedges & grasses.

Oeneis chryxus

Chryxus Arctic

LIFESTYLE... 1 brood. White eggs. Winters as young multi-striped caterpillar, sometimes taking 2 years to mature. Light brown chrysalis with darker head.

Moist mountain meadows. Often near aspens.

Common Alpine

Erebia epipsodea

LIFESTYLE... I brood. Single or small groups of pale round eggs. Winters as young green-striped caterpillar among leaves silked together. Brownish chrysalis.

HOST... grasses & sedges.

NECTAR... Yellow composites & mud.

Adaptability brings farthest south.

LIFESTYLE... I brood. Pale yellow-ridged eggs. Winters as young, yellow-lined, fuzzy, two red-tailed green caterpillar. (Got that?)

Plump green chrysalis. Highly variable with many aliases.

Skillfully navigates through **HOST...** tall grasses.

Common Wood Nymph

Cercyonis pegala

Coreopsis

WS 2-3"

FAVORS... Grassy woodland edges & marshes.

More satyrs...

NECTAR... occasionally ironweed, fleabane, mint, & females on rotting fruits.

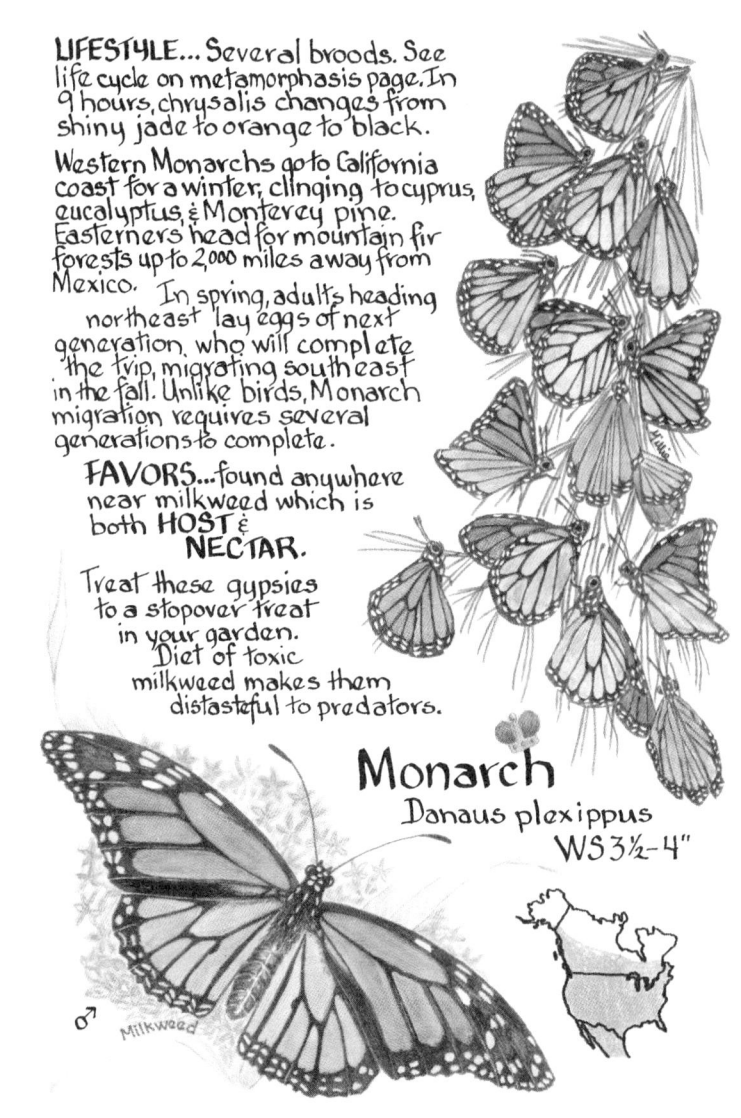

LIFESTYLE... Several broods. See life cycle on metamorphasis page. In 9 hours, chrysalis changes from shiny jade to orange to black.

Western Monarchs go to California coast for a winter, clinging to cyprus, eucalyptus & Monterey pine. Easterners head for mountain fir forests up to 2,000 miles away from Mexico. In spring, adults heading northeast lay eggs of next generation, who will complete the trip, migrating southeast in the fall. Unlike birds, Monarch migration requires several generations to complete.

FAVORS... found anywhere near milkweed which is both **HOST** & **NECTAR**.

Treat these gypsies to a stopover treat in your garden. Diet of toxic milkweed makes them distasteful to predators.

Monarch
Danaus plexippus
WS 3½ - 4"

♂   Milkweed

Queen
Danaus gilippus

See caterpillar on cover.

LIFESTYLE... Several broods. Pale oval eggs. Gold-spotted green chrysalis. Migrates south for the winter. Another distasteful Milkweed that's mimicked by darker form of Viceroy.

WS 3-3½"

During courtship, all male Milkweed butterflies transfer scents first from hindwings to abdominal "hair pencils" & then to female antennae. Their-fore, play like this is required by females for mating.

FAVORS... Open places with HOST... milkweeds.

NECTAR... milkweeds, fogfruit, & daisies.

Viceroy
Basilarchia archippus
WS 2½-3"

LIFESTYLE... 3+ broods. Pale green or yellow eggs. Larva winter hidden in leaf shreddings. This tasty jester mimics both Monarch in the North & Queen in the South for protection from predators.

FAVORS... shrubby waterways.

HOST... prefers willows, poplar, & aspen... sometimes fruit trees in rose family.

NECTAR... tree sap, carrion, dung, aphid honeydew, & rotting fruit plus thistle, aster, & goldenrod.

A camouflage magician.

Milkweeds and Mimic

White Admiral
Basilarchia arthemis arthemis

WS 3-3¼"

FAVORS... deciduous forest edges.

HOST... birches, willows, & poplars.

NECTAR... carrion, running sap, rotting fruit,

LIFESTYLE... 1-2 broods. Greenish eggs. Winters as caterpillar on host trees, rolled in a leaf tied with silk. Emerges ravenous in spring. Pale chrysalis has dark patches.

aphid honeydew, dung, & flowers.

"Banded Purple" males attack territory invaders.

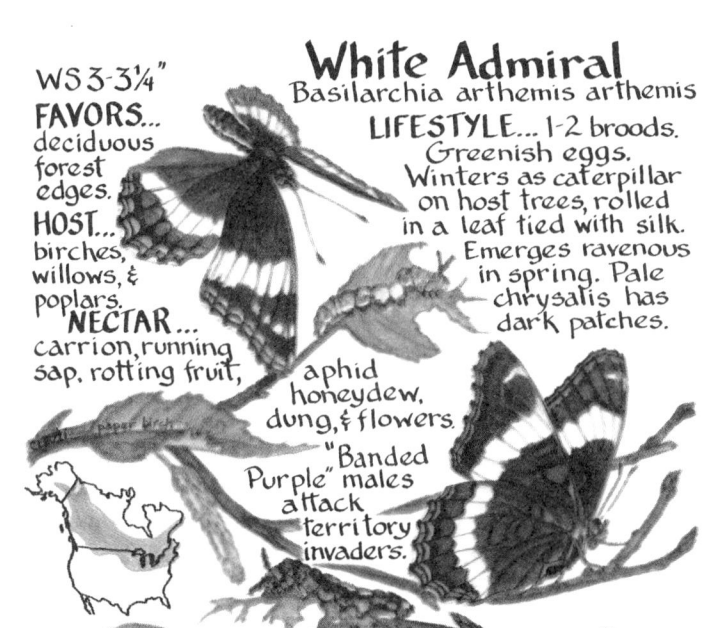

paper birch

Red-spotted Purple
Basilarchia arthemis astyanax

Often inter-breed with White Admiral. Mimics bad-tasting Pipevine to protect self from hungry birds but risks it to bask on a sunny sidewalk.

LIFESTYLE... 2-3 broods. Grayish green eggs. Winters as cater-pillar.

FAVORS... meadows, water-ways, & woodland edges.

WS 3-3½"

HOST... willow, poplar, aspen, fruit & hawthorn trees plus gooseberry bushes.
NECTAR... same as White Admiral plus cardinal flowers, viburnem, & spirea.

WS 2¾ – 3½"

Weidemeyer's Admiral
Basilarchia weidemeyerii

LIFESTYLE... 1 brood. Greenish eggs. Chrysalis & caterpillar resemble bird droppings. Winters as young caterpillar. Sails Rocky Mt. canyons & deciduous woodlands up to 11,000 feet.

HOST... aspens & willows.

NECTAR... similar to White Admiral.

FAVORS... perches on trees & shrubs of slopes & waterways. Patrols edges of aspen groves.

California Sister
Adelpha bredowii

WS 3-3½"

LIFESTYLE... 2 broods. Spherical eggs. Winters as young caterpillar. Light beige humpbacked chrysalis. Named after a nun's habit.

FAVORS... oak woods & wet canyons. A puddler.

NECTAR... overripe fruit & buckeye flowers. A grape juice taster at wineries.

HOST... oaks.

Admirals & Sisters

LIFESTYLE... 3 or more broods. Tiny yellow eggs. Like lemmings, "skip" north in years of over-population.

WS 1½-2"

Long-tailed

Urbanus proteus

FAVORS... waterways & gardens.

NECTAR... lantana, composites, & many other flowers.

HOST... legumes. A pest to bean farmers.

Chrysalis dusted with 4x sugar.

Epargyreus clarus

Silver-spotted

WS 1¾-2½"

LIFESTYLE... 1-3 broods. Green eggs. Loose silken cocoon covers chrysalis in ground litter. Feisty... darting or skipping out to inspect travelers. Sleep hanging... *upside down*.

Males can put on great aerial displays.

FAVORS... Extensive land
from open wet forest to
parks & gardens.

HOST... locust & other legumes,
wisteria, & beggar's tick.

NECTAR... honeysuckle, iris, red
clover, butterfly
weed, zinnia, &
Joe-Pye weed.

Caterpillars
curl up in
shelters of
tightly spun legume
leaves to winter.

Golden Pea

Northern Cloudywing

Thorybes
pylades

LIFESTYLE... 1 or more
broods. Light green eggs.
Colorful pink/purple/green
caterpillar makes silk nest
in legume leaves.

Hibernates the
winter as full-
grown caterpillar.

FAVORS... Clearings
& woodland edges.

NECTAR... dogbane,
milkweed, thistles, red
clover, & vetch. Prefer
white, pink, purple, & blue
flowers. Avoid yellow,
orange, & red.

Joe-Pye weed

WS 1¼ - 1¾"

HOST... beggar tick & several legumes.

Herb, Shrub, & Tree Skippers

Aptly named
Skippers differ from true butterflies with larger
bodies, smaller wings, & hooked antennae. Mothlike.

WS 3/4 - 1¼"

NECTAR...
aster, fleabane, knapweed, and red clover.

FAVORS...
Weedy foothills & prairies, vacant lots, gardens, and parks.

Pyrgus communis

Checkered

LIFESTYLE... Many broods. Eggs change from green to cream before hatching. Tan caterpillar has dark lines & head. Dashing speckled chrysalis greener at head & browner at tip. Winters as either.

HOST...
mallows & hollyhock

Adult coloration variable. Aggressive males patrol actively for females.
Short fast flight.

Aster

Common Sooty Wing

Pholisora catullus

WS 1-1¼"

NECTAR... common milkweed, marjoram, peppermint, white clover, & dogbane.

FAVORS... weedy, disturbed areas & gardens.

HOST... pigweed, cheeseweed, goosefoot, & lambs quarters (Yum! Yum!).

LIFESTYLE... 2-3 broods. Teensy yellowish eggs. Winters in leaf tent as flecked, striped green caterpillar with dark head. Purplish chrysalis, hairy except on wing cases.

Dogbane

Sleepy Dusky Wing

Erynnis brizo

LIFESTYLE... 1-2 broods. Green eggs. Winters as speckled, hairy, green caterpillar with reddish head. Green chrysalis.

FAVORS... Foothills & shrubby areas.

HOST... variety of oaks or chestnuts.

WS...1⅛-1½"

NECTAR... favors heath flowers, such as azalea and blueberries; also blackberries & dandelion.

Blackberry

More Herb, Shrub, & Tree **Skippers**

Least

Ancyloxypha numitor

LIFESTYLE...
2-4 broods. Shiny yellow eggs. Winters as older green caterpillar with brown head. Brown & white chrysalis.

HOST... grasses, marsh millet, bluegrass, and rice.

NECTAR... low plants with small flowers, such as clover, wood sorrels, & vetches.

WS ¾-1"

WS 1-1¼"

FAVORS... along streams & moist grassy places.

switchgrass

Listen for him zipping across the lawn.

FAVORS... grassy lawns, glades, & roadsides.

HOST... bent, crab, bermuda, St. Augustine, & sugarcane grasses.

Fiery

Hylephila phyleus

LIFESTYLE... 2 or more broods. Turquoise eggs. Tan caterpillar has 3 long stripes & builds shelter at grass base to escape lawnmowers. Lighter chrysalis has 1 stripe. In winter, adults play in deep South.

NECTAR... lantana, aster, swamp milkweed, thistle, & ironweed.

St. augustine

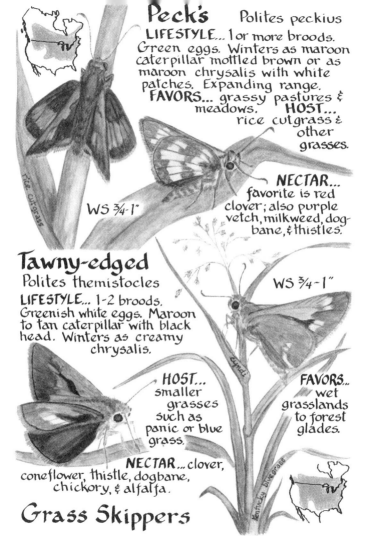

Peck's
Polites peckius

LIFESTYLE... 1 or more broods. Green eggs. Winters as maroon caterpillar mottled brown or as maroon chrysalis with white patches. Expanding range.

FAVORS... grassy pastures & meadows.

HOST... rice cutgrass & other grasses.

NECTAR... favorite is red clover; also purple vetch, milkweed, dogbane, & thistles.

WS ¾-1"

rice cutgrass

Tawny-edged
Polites themistocles

LIFESTYLE... 1-2 broods. Greenish white eggs. Maroon to tan caterpillar with black head. Winters as creamy chrysalis.

WS ¾-1"

HOST... smaller grasses such as panic or blue grass.

FAVORS... wet grasslands to forest glades.

NECTAR... clover, coneflower, thistle, dogbane, chickory, & alfalfa.

Kentucky bluegrass

Grass Skippers

Dun

Euphyes vestris

LIFESTYLE...

1-2 broods.
Pale green eggs become red tipped before hatching.
Winters as silvery green caterpillar.
Yellow to green hairy chrysalis.
Males lack tiny light spots, but some have orange heads. **FAVORS...**
mountain sides, woods, & pastures.
NECTAR...
white, pink, & purple flowers, especially mints, fireweed, dogbane, purple vetch, & lotus.

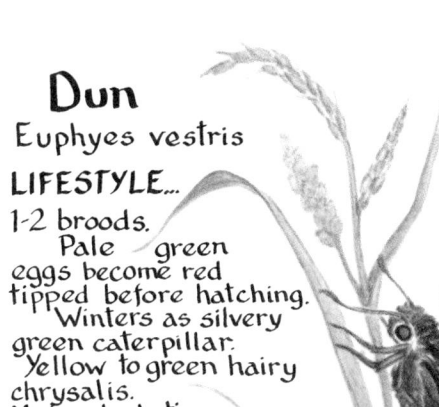

WS 1-1¼"
♀

HOST...
sedges.

WS 1-1½"
♀

Hobomok

Poanes hobomok

LIFESTYLE... 1 brood.
Pale green eggs.
Winters as dark green caterpillar or chrysalis.
FAVORS... deciduous woods, paths, & meadows.

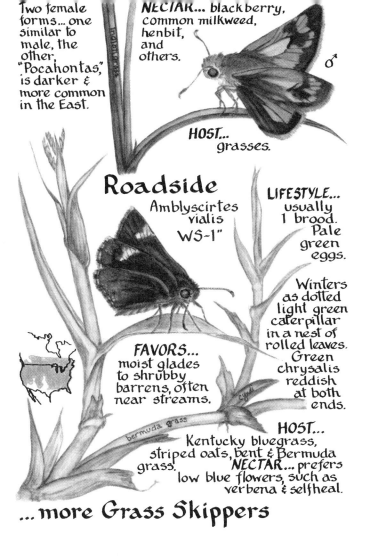

Two female forms... one similar to male, the other, "Pocahontas," is darker & more common in the East.

NECTAR... blackberry, common milkweed, henbit, and others.

Italian grass

♂

HOST... grasses.

Roadside

Amblyscirtes vialis
WS~1"

LIFESTYLE... usually 1 brood. Pale green eggs.

Winters as dotted light green caterpillar in a nest of rolled leaves. Green chrysalis reddish at both ends.

FAVORS... moist glades to shrubby barrens, often near streams.

HOST... Kentucky bluegrass, striped oats, bent & Bermuda grass.
NECTAR... prefers low blue flowers, such as verbena & selfheal.

bermuda grass

... more Grass Skippers

The Blue Ribbon
goes to the amazing
Boyce Drummond Ph.D.
whose energetic support
enabled the metamorphosis
of this project.
Lad, you've won First Prize!

Special thanks to
Karie Darrow, who shared
our enthusiasm at the
butterfly drawers of the
University of Colorado Museum.

For more information,
contact your local
Lepidopterists' Society, or
The Xerces Society
10 Southwest Ash St.
Portland, Or 97204

Colorado Hairstreak
Hypaurotis
crysalus
WS 1¼-1½"

Dedication... to
Jeffrey and Christina,
my youngest flutterbys,
May your fondest
dreams sprout wings!
        Love always,
            Mom

references...

Mitchell, Robert T & Herbert
S. Zim. Butterflies and Moths.
New York: Golden Press, 1987.

Pyle, Robert Michael. The
Audubon Society Field Guide
to North American Butterflies.
New York: Chanticleer Press,
Inc., 1992.

Schneck, Marcus. Butter-
flies: How to Identify & Attract
Them to Your Garden. Emmaus,
Pa : Rodale Press, 1990.

Stokes, Donald & Lillian and
Ernest Williams. The Butter-
fly Book, An Easy Guide to
Butterfly Gardening, Ident-
ification, & Behavior. Boston:
Little, Brown & Co., 1991.

The Xerces Society
in association with The
Smithsonian Institution.
Butterfly Gardening:
Creating Summer Magic
in Your Garden. San
Francisco: Sierra Club
Books, 1990.

For consistency, all butterfly names taken from...

Miller, Jacqueline Y.
The Common Names of North
American Butterflies. Wash-
ington, D.C.: Smithsonian
Institution Press, 1992.